SEX
in the Pews

J.K. SANDERS

SEX IN THE PEWS

Copyright ©2013 by Jonathan K. Sanders
www.jksandersministries.org

Unless otherwise noted, all scripture quotations are taken from the King James Version of the Holy Bible.

ISBN: 978-0-615-90218-0
Printed in the United States of America

Book design by Cheryl Holland
A'Sista Media Group, LLC
www.asistamedia .com

DEDICATION

This book is dedicated to anyone that has been offended by an act of sex by a member that claimed to be a representative of the church. I want you to know that you can be delivered. Everything that happened to you is simply part of your testimony.

ACKNOWLEDGEMENTS

To those who influenced me the most, Bishop Fred and the late Mother Esther Sanders, I offer the most sincere gratitude. The words you spoke continue to speak in my spirit and remind me that this is just the beginning.

To my wonderful sons, Jonathan and Joshua, you bring me joy. The world awaits you as you've been waiting on it. Continue to prove to me that you are the men your mother and I raised.

INTRODUCTION

SEX IN THE PEWS…Yes, it might as well be! This book is an exposé on the so-called hidden sex culture in the church. To those of you that have been in church for years, I won't say anything that is surprising to you. You know the real from the fake. Those on the outside will look at the title on this book and believe I'm talking out of my head because they haven't experienced the inside circuit. I conducted various interviews while researching and completing this book. However, I have personally experienced some of the indiscretions you will read in this book.

I've been in ministry for 23 years. For 17 of those years, I traveled all over the world including places like California, Nevada, New York, and Washington, DC. I have traveled internationally, as well, preaching the gospel in Canada, Jamaica, British Virgin Islands, Guyana, Barbados, and Trinidad. The things I have witnessed down through the years have been quite shocking and would have caused the average brother to stop preaching and get a white-collar job downtown! I was born on the pew as the "Mothers' Board" would say! As a PK (preacher kid), my dad was preaching and pastoring before I could walk or talk. Growing up with a dad who was also my pastor, I knew some experiences came with the territory.

The Bible is filled with sexual innuendos and issues. The great King David saw a woman so fine, named Bathsheba, that he slept with her. Then, he killed her husband Uriah. Another great man, Solomon, had 300 wives and another 700 concubines. Samson's heart was broken because his father-in-law gave his new wife to his best man. This episode caused him to chase women trying to fill a void. Judah slept with his own daughter-in-law, Tamar, impregnating her. She disguised herself as a prostitute, so he didn't have a clue. When he heard she was pregnant, he told the people to burn a sister up! Isn't that a trip? When she proved he was her baby's daddy, he had to apologize and said she had been more righteous than he was. A man in the book of Corinthians was sleeping with his own father's wife! I can go on and on but the Bible itself is filled with…Sex in the Pews!

This book was not written to embarrass or call out anybody, so no names will be mentioned. I have changed names and locations to protect identities. I have conducted interviews, personally experienced some things, and prayed often about this book. This book is not a compilation of all church people and their behaviors. This book is not exemplary of all church environments, pastors, preachers, evangelists or any member of church leadership. In my 23 years of walking with Christ, I have been guilty of some of the very same things that I'm writing about in this book. Thank God that through the redemptive blood of Jesus Christ, He has forgiven and strengthened me. I'm not perfect, but I certainly am delivered!

To some this may be fictional, but to others this is real. In this book I will simply write publicly what others say in private. I am a strong believer of the scripture in *John 8:32, "And ye shall know the truth, and the truth shall make you free."* My father always told me that if you are a true preacher you must always speak the truth, even if you have to step on your own toes! The sad reality is people know that this is happening in the house of God, but will act like they don't know. If you can't handle the truth, this is a good time to put this book down. To the brave, bold, and daring, let's enter into what I call the "real zone"!

TABLE OF CONTENTS

WARNING

Can you handle the truth?

You would think that church would be the place where you would never hear lies and always hear the truth. Sadly, you are greatly mistaken. More lies are told in the pulpit than you would ever believe. People say they want the truth, but in reality they can't handle the truth. As a young man I wanted to know why people lied from the pulpit. As I matured I realized that people actually want to hear something that they like and want. Back in the day we had old school pastors who didn't care about opinions of people, because they knew they were called to preach the truth. In today's culture, it is the complete opposite. Today, pastors are trying to be superstars and obtain a mega church. They are saying whatever it takes to pack the pews and offering baskets. They will tell you what they think will get you to shout, dance, and keep coming back. Now, I'm not saying that the preacher should make you feel bad when you come to church, but you should always get the truth at all costs. Yes the church will be packed when the preacher is telling the people what they want to hear, but the question is who is packing the church. Is the church packed with people that are trying to be saved and live right or is it packed with people that simply want to be entertained? Any preacher or pastor that will play with your soul is a dangerous individual! God said it clearly in His Word.

> *"Cry aloud and spare not, lift up thy voice like a trumpet, and shew my people their transgression and the house of Jacob their sins." Isaiah 58:1 KJV*

God wanted preachers to never abandon their job of telling the truth and to always be bold with it.

Sexually Transmitted Demons (STDs)

Have you ever heard the statement, "If you lay down with dogs you will get up with fleas?" Guess what? It is a true statement. Never underestimate a single act of sex because there is more exchanged in that moment than just body fluids. Emotions, characteristics, and even spirits are exchanged. Have you ever known two people who were sexually involved, and then suddenly one began acting just like the other? Sex is a powerful act. It is more than you can really see or understand. During sex, dark spirits are involved and you may find yourself getting up out of that bed with something inside of you that wasn't there before. I knew of a chick who was a Christian and she started kicking it with a Muslim. Eventually, she switched religions! I don't know what happened in that room, but sexually transmitted demons are no joke! All I'm saying is demonic spirits can transfer themselves to others through the act of sex. How do you think a man that has nothing can sleep with a woman that has everything and in a matter of days he is living with her, driving her car, and soon she is putting his name on her credit cards? Don't tell me it is just an isolated act of sex! Most women know this goes against how they've been raised. It goes against their common sense, but they can't help themselves. I've learned to be very compassionate and understanding of situations like this because when spirits take over a person, his or her common sense goes straight out the window. Trust me on this one because I have seen it too many times. All of us have heard of cases when a woman is involved with a man who is verbally and physically abusive, but she just won't leave. Her mom and girlfriends have pleaded with her, but for some reason she stays right by his side like a loyal german shepherd. This is called a sexually transmitted demon (STD), my friends. I personally believe that some people are demonically possessed with an acquired set of sex skills that when someone sleeps with them they gain total control of that individual. If you don't believe me, allow your mind to go down memory lane. Think about your own life and how certain sexual relations occurred. What was it that made you get up out of your own comfortable bed in the wee hours of the morning? Why did you give them your hard earned money? Why did you believe them when you knew in your heart they were not being truthful? The list can go on and on, especially for those of us that will be honest. Remember, true deliverance only comes when you speak the truth and are honest with yourself. Even a liar wants to be told the truth!

It's more common than you think

This subject of sex in the pews goes beyond one religion. From Catholic priests to Pentecostal pastors, no one is exempt in the wild church sex culture. Even at the Kingdom Hall and Mosques, there are indiscretions that would shock and amaze you. This spirit can be found in all religions and denominations, so I caution you to not be judgmental. The devil will use anybody and can get within anybody who will let him in. Let's take a look at Judas. Even after serving with Jesus and seeing Him raise the dead and heal countless people, Judas still let the devil use him. How someone could walk with the Master for three and a half years and allow the devil in is absolutely unreal. We've probably seen more news coverage on Catholic priests molesting boys than any other religion, but it is certainly not just happening in their religious communities. As a matter of fact, we are partly being desensitized because it is so common today. Ask people around you if you don't believe me. I'm not spreading bad news because it does a good job of traveling fast by itself. I warn people about these things all the time because I don't like when people look at the church like it is a place of perfection. The church is certainly far from perfection.

Hell is everywhere, and if you read your Bible you will see that even hell broke out in heaven when Lucifer staged a coup. Eventually his coup got him put out of heaven. Consequently if somebody was put out of heaven surely somebody will get put out of church. We'll get into that later. Pray for your church at all times, especially your pastor. It may sound cliché, but at the end of the day, he or she is still just a human being.

You would be surprised to learn how many people would fall out with you if you simply told them the truth. This is what happened to so many in the Bible when they gave the people of God the truth. When you are an advocate of the truth, you don't gain friends. Instead, you gain enemies. Maybe that is why many don't speak the unadulterated truth! The Apostle Paul wrote:

> *"Am I therefore become your enemy, because I tell you the truth?" Galatians 4:16 KJV*

Can you believe that? He is not talking to sinners, but he is talking to members of his own church that he founded. It is similar to a child not wanting to hear the truth from his or her parent! The truth is not in demand as much as you may think, and sad to say not even in church.

CHAPTER

MARRIAGES OF CONVENIENCE

Cover me and I'll cover you

This is a very sensitive subject so I'll tread lightly. Then again, no I won't! Let me keep it real and give you the truth. The Bible says:

> *"Marriage is honorable in all, and the bed undefiled: but whoremongers and adulterers God will judge."*
> *Hebrews 13:4 KJV*

Marriage also looks good on leadership in the church, especially those sitting in the pulpit. Husband, wife, son, and daughter can look like the picture perfect role model of a family. The sad part is, in some cases, it is nothing more than a front. I can speak personally on this because I'm a single pastor. I recognize that if I got married, my church would attract more family units. I've been greatly pressured by my peers to marry for this exact reason. Yet I have never given into that because if I marry it is not going to be because I want more members at my church, but because I'm in love and she is my Queen to be! Today there are pastors that are in an arranged relationship based on business, not love. If the pastor is full of lust, he or she will marry someone but they will let their spouse know in the beginning that it is an open relationship. There are so many people that want to be in that position of influence that they will accept any terms. They know that these positions come with some level of "material comfort" like a nice car and a decent place to stay. I personally know of first ladies that know their husband/pastor is cheating with women, but because they get to live in a huge house, drive an imported car, and have a good weekly stipend; they gladly look the other way. There are a lot of women that are cool with it. Why? Most likely, the first lady is banging the church musician! Yes, I said it!

The perfect front…they will never know

When people are married, they are supposed to have each other's back. In the case we are about to discuss, they certainly do. There are some church leaders who are living the gay life and married! Yes, I said it. It is no way in the world that their companion doesn't know. Come on! Let's be real! Some of these individuals are flaming so bright that you know they are gay a mile and three quarters away. Now I'm not picking at anyone, so don't trip on me. There are some leaders that are homosexual with a lesbian wife, so the code is lie for me and I'll lie for you. Have you ever seen a married church pastor and you knew he or she was gay? You tried to believe it wasn't true because you knew they were married. I know you have! That is one of the craziest scenarios to me. I'm not saying if he or she is gay that the companion is too, but that scenario is prevalent. Trust me! I've always wondered how is it that a spouse can stay with a companion and they themselves know that their companion is gay. What makes them stay? I don't know. I do know that the position of a pastor's spouse, whether it is male or female, is a mighty strong position to many people. Some would kill to get in that position and will do whatever it takes! The spouse would lie for his or her companion in any scenario they are in because they don't want to lose that position of prestige. They will say their spouse is faithful, not gay, or whatever it takes because they don't want to lose their position.

CHAPTER

FREAKS IN THE CHURCH!
(PEDOPHILES AND MOLESTERS)

Leave those kids alone!

This is a very sensitive subject because we are talking about the precious children who are our future. So many kids have been molested, not just at a relative's house, day-care, or school, but also in church. You have seen stories on the news and have read it on the Internet of how children have had their innocence taken in the house of God. This is preposterous to say the least! A violent sexual act should never happen to any child, but for it to happen in the house of God by someone who says they represent Him is crazy. Bishop, apostle, deacon, elder, and missionary are a few of the titles that the undercover freaks use to win the confidence and trust of unsuspecting children. I tell people all the time that it is one thing to have wolves in sheep's clothing, but when you have shepherds in wolves' clothing you have a hot mess on your hands! No one with a sexual deviant past should be over the children in the church. As a matter of fact, it is not a bad idea to do a background check because the church can be sued for the lewd acts of one of its leaders. If you're a freak like that, leave these damn kids alone! I believe there is a special place in hell for people like that. The sad thing is that these leaders are even protected by their members because of their influence over them. When a person protects someone that they know is doing illegal sex acts to kids, he or she should be a cellmate of that individual.

There is quite a difference between a molester and a pedophile. The raw truth of it is that not all pedophiles are molesters and vice versa. Pedophilia is a diagnosable disorder where the perpetrator has an attraction to children. A molester is one who touches a child in a sexual manner. As crazy as it sounds, pedophilia is a mental disorder and not illegal. To date, no cure has been discovered. I don't want to go too far left on this, but couldn't a person like this be demon possessed? Can an individual not have mental illness at all, but be full of the devil? I'll save that until my next point.

Can they be delivered?

This is a very intriguing question and the answer changes depending upon whom you ask. To those who have been molested, they would tell you absolutely not! The victims will tell you about how many years this person caused havoc and confusion in their lives distorting their sexual preference. To a victim, he or she sees relief if pain comes to the tormentors along with a lifelong prison sentence. Sadly, victims carry so much pain that all they want is the wrath of God to come down on the perpetrator.

To say that a molester or pedophile can't be delivered is saying that the power of God is limited. You and I know that the blood of Jesus can redeem and He will forgive anyone of whatever sin they've committed. Never let this incident make you so mean and cruel, because you are the victim, that you no longer believe in the power of our Christ. Yes, they can be delivered if they have a heart to change and turn their lives around. It is just the same as a person that has been a thief, liar, crack head, or whoremonger and their life changes because they receive Christ. How can you then say a child molester can't change? That is nuts and rather ridiculous, to say the least. I know that it's easier said than done, but it can be done. You can forgive that individual and release them to receive God's redemptive power. Yes they can be forgiven, but we must be a people that will let them know it can be done. The position of the church and church people is to never give up on anybody. The word of God clearly teaches what Jesus said.

> *"Come unto me, all ye that labour and are heavy laden, and I will give you rest." Matthew 11:28 KJV*

If you want my personal opinion on the question about deliverance, my answer is absolutely!

Should they be in church or just prison?

Who is the judge of who is allowed to come in the church and who has to stay out? What margins do we use? Do we let liars in and keep hoes out (male and female)? Do we say the whoremongers and fornicators can stay but kick the pedophiles and molesters out? Who gives us that right? If that is what we use to decide who is allowed in and who has to stay out, we must speak on all sin. If they can't come to church and get themselves together, where else can they go? On another note, do you really think they are getting deliverance or the therapy they need behind prison bars? Of course for a crime they should serve their time, but what about when they get out? Secondly, do you think a crime or sin such as this is the absolute worst? You know everyone has an opinion of what they think is good, bad, or horrible. Let me end it like this! What if the pedophile or molester was your dad or brother? Wouldn't you want them to be given a second chance? I rest my case in the jury's hands.

CHAPTER

WHO OPENED THE GATE AND LET THIS SPIRIT IN?

Preachers that won't preach the truth

How did the church get so buck wild? Growing up as a child in New York in a Pentecostal church, you knew that you were in church at all times. There were simply some things that you didn't hear or see in church. People had great respect for the house of God and the man or woman of God. Not any more! People will say or do whatever they want in church just like they do at the mall. It is not a strange thing to hear about folks having sex in church! It is one thing to meet somebody at church, but to have the audacity to screw in God's house is crazy. I don't know about you, but even if I was married I couldn't conceptualize the thought of getting jiggy in the house of the Lord. Now that is my conviction! I know freaks will do it on planes, trains, and automobiles. My dad always told me when I first started preaching back in 1991, "Son, I may be dead and gone, but remember weak preaching produces weak saints." That has always stayed in my mind as I ministered and now even the more as a pastor. It is never the minister's job to tell you what you want to hear, but instead to tell you what God has said, whether you like it or not.

Who let this crazy sex spirit in church? You got it! It was the preachers and pastors! A lot of mess in church starts in the pulpit. Not in all cases, but certainly most. Homosexuals will fill up a church fast, especially if the pastor is gay. Hoes will run to a church where the pastor is a hoe whether they are male or female.

The good old preacher's club says I'm not supposed to tell you this. A great deal of pastors won't preach on sin because they know people don't really want to hear it. The crooked preacher let this spirit in because he or she wants to be famous and popular. How can a church be packed with fornicators, but the pastor never preaches on fornication? Do you think God is blind? Now, hear me clearly! I'm not saying that the pastor should start rebuking and sending everybody to hell, but he or she should preach on that spirit in love. In Jeremiah 31:3 God said with loving kindness have I drawn thee. This new generation doesn't want to hear about their sins and issues. They want to be entertained and that is what the wicked preacher is giving them. Whenever a minister chooses not to give the people the truth, he or she is literally playing with their souls. I pray you are not in a church where your pastor is telling you lies and only what you want to hear. If you are, get the hell out!

Saints in the pews who control the pulpit

You ask how in the world can people in the pews control the pulpit? They do it easily with their attendance and especially their money. As a pastor you have certain members in your church who are what they call big givers. These big givers, at times, seem to want to be able to control the preacher because they give a lot. This is even stronger in churches where the pastor is controlled by a board that pays their salary. I've heard horror stories from some of my pastor friends on how the board would jerk them around financially. If the preacher preaches happy go lucky sermons that make the people dance, their salary rises. If the preacher gives them a stern Word and preaches against sin and people get upset, they will get a decrease in salary. That is crazy, especially, since God should have given him that sermon.

I am in no way saying preachers shouldn't uplift the people with a joyous word, but sometimes God leads you a different way. There have been times when God gave me a sermon and I thought to myself, "Oh boy it's going to be a rough Sunday!" There are some saints that control the pulpit by their looks at the preacher. They will look at you crazy if you're preaching on something that they don't want to hear. You'd be surprised at the looks we get from the people in the pews when we're saying something they don't want to hear. If you are a weak minister that can't handle the faces of the people, you are in trouble in this season.

God told His preacher:

> *"As an adamant harder than flint have I made thy forehead: fear them not, neither be dismayed at their looks, though they be a rebellious house."*
> *Ezekiel 3:9 KJV*

In other words He said don't fear those folks, but preach on anyway! Preachers, can you be bold enough to do what God said without a hundred amens and a few thousand hallelujahs? Don't let anybody fool you! Real preachers are bold and are not bothered by stank faces, and I'm one of them.

How to pack out a church in 90 days

Ministry today is very complex. So many people want to be a pastor because it looks glorious to them and they think it's financially rewarding to the point where you don't have to work. Well, they are sadly mistaken! It is so hard for some churches to get members that some scoundrels in the pulpit have gotten thirsty enough to get a bag and fill it up with tricks. They pack churches out by letting a little bit of everything go on in their churches. People sleeping with one another, having swingers' parties, going to clubs after church, getting high and drunk together so in reality it's not a church, but a social club! Everybody covers up for each other and it becomes a big private club and the only way you get in is you have to do what everybody else is doing, and of course keep your mouth closed!

One of the other tricks preachers use to pack out a church is to have what is called a prophetic revival. Now, let me first say this. I greatly believe in the prophetic, just not the pathetic! Some of these so-called prophets couldn't hear God speak if he had a bullhorn to their ear! They come to different cities under the guise of "prophet" proclaiming they can raise a lot of money. If the pastor is struggling, he will certainly call them to preach.

Don't believe everything you hear. Carefully weigh and

examine what people tell you. Not everyone who talks about God comes from God. It says in 1 John 4:1 that there are a lot of lying preachers running loose in the world. The most common prophetic lie you hear in church today is "God is about to bless you with a husband" or "God is getting ready to bless you with a house". Why are these two false prophecies so common in church? That is easy, the church is predominately filled with women and they are mostly working women!

Most women want a husband and because they are career-oriented, they greatly desire a nice house. The poor pastor stands there surprised, thinking, "This person doesn't even pay tithes and they're getting all of this?" Sadly, male prophets, especially, tell women that untruth because when the women are happy about a future they think is coming, here comes the big offering! Oops, did I say that? Yes, I did but that is a whole different chapter. How in the Mahaliah Jackson is God going to bless you with a house and you don't even pay rent for a one bedroom on time? How is he going to bless some women with a husband and they are not even wifey material? You do know that according to Proverbs that a woman is a wife even *before* she gets married, don't you?

> "Whoso findeth a wife findeth a good thing, and obtaineth favour of the Lord." Proverbs 18:22 KJV

Notice that the woman is a wife before the man even found her. If I can't help you, I sure won't hurt you.

Lastly, one of the other ways they pack out a church is by

making the unsuspecting new member believe that they have a romantic future with them. This tactic works on some women whether the preacher is married or not. The single pastor would tell women or men that in the future I can see us married, but right now the Lord wants us to do all we can to build this ministry. They will take you out here and there and spend time with you, but watch this, you can't tell anybody! They'll tell you that they keep their business personal, but in reality they have told other members the exact same thing so they have to kick it on the low. Tight, but its right! I've seen people stay in ministry like this for years, only to be left holding the trick bag and the pastor marries somebody else or remains single.

To me, that is a terrible thing to do to a person when all along you don't have good intentions toward them. When you play with someone's heart like that, it is a low down dirty shame. Let me add this statement right here. I am a single pastor. I have and still do date, but I have never lied and deceived any woman about my future aspirations with her to get her to keep pushing my ministry. My mother always told me, "Son never string a woman along and play with her feelings. If you do that, God will punish you. But rather tell her the truth especially if she asks you. If she asks you if you love her, tell her the truth. If she asks you if you see you two married or in a relationship, tell her the truth. If you do this son, God will bless you and your ministry." At the writing of this book, my mother has been gone for less than a year yet her words still ring from the grave to my ears. I never will do that to a sister who could have possibly married somebody else and went on with her life. The negative side of being brutally honest is that feelings get hurt. I've had women ask me what do I think about them and as nice as I try to say it, some really go off on me, to say the least! I've been cursed out, some have spread rumors about me, while a few are cool enough to say thank you for being honest. Any real seasoned woman would tell another woman that you better thank God for a man that will tell you the truth, even when it's not in your favor.

It's really not that different for pastors that are married, yet string others along. They will tell you how horrible their companion is but they still stay with them. This can keep a church packed, especially if you have some thirsty men or women in that church. They will almost wait until Jesus comes for you to get a divorce. The sad part is they usually treat the first lady or the female pastor's husband very cruel. The sad thing is the poor spouse doesn't have a clue why they are getting such harsh treatment. I know very few first ladies that really enjoy being one. Now please keep your thinking caps on friends because I'm obviously not talking about all pastors or all churches. You have some really great examples of true love in the house of God. However, there are those that want the position of the spouse of the pastor and so they treat the current spouse badly. At times, the pastor has no control over a lot of it. If pastors openly let their members disrespect and speak evil of their spouse, you better watch out because something is suspect about that. I'm certainly not saying that they should put every person like this out of the church, but the person certainly should be dealt with and told that kind of behavior won't be tolerated. You can bet your baby toe that when a male pastor has a great deal of women in his church disrespecting and belittling his wife for years and he does nothing about it, trust me, he is banging a few of them! Yes, I said it again! The church is packed out, but packed with what? That's the question that should be asked.

CHAPTER

I'M GOING TO GET THAT BY ANY MEANS NECESSARY

You joined the church but who sent you?

There is not a pastor alive that doesn't like to preach to a jam-packed church. It's like a feeling of great accomplishment. We are ready to preach the hell out of the message that morning when the church is filled to capacity. It feels like a mother who cooked all day, set the table, and now she's sitting back watching the kids tear that food up.

The question must be asked. Who sent you to the ministry? You haven't been around long if you think that God sent everybody that joins the church. There are people that join churches for all kinds of reasons. Some join to get business opportunities, like clients for their hair salon. Besides, you and I know, there's more weave at church than it is at the Chinese store! Lol. Sorry I had to. There are others that join the church because there are good-looking men or beautiful women. Some join just to be social and get out of the house, never tapping into the spiritual side of what church is all about.

Then, there is the plan of the devil to send people into the church to tear it down! The devil sends Jezebels with the attempt to screw everything that isn't nailed down. These new age Jezebels are absolutely drop dead gorgeous from their heads to their toes. They smell like a perfume that costs a thousand dollars a bottle! Don't let anybody fool you! The preacher man, tax man, and the doctor man are attracted to beauty. It's all about what you do with it. As one preacher said, "Nothing's wrong with looking at the menu as long as you don't order nothing." Lol. Back to Jezebel or should I say Jezehell. When this kind of woman joins a church, she has only one intention and that is to tear it apart. She will get active, sing on the praise team, and give good money. If it's a pastor that is motivated by finances, he won't put her out of the church for her shenanigans. Marriages will be destroyed and attitudes will start surfacing because Jezebel has been working overtime screwing, sucking, and manipulating. It will take a real pastor to deal with this kind of spirit because she is smoother than silk and it will take strong discernment to see how the devil is working. Most churches have already encountered this spirit so what I'm saying is nothing strange to them. If you have a Jezebel in your church, I pray you get her the hell out of there before it is too late.

Social media freaks! (Facebook, Twitter, Instagram)

The Internet is almost like a ministry in and of itself. Most churches have a television program and you can watch all of their services from your tablet or cell phone. Because of social media, a lot of ministries have members all over the world. There is really no danger to this with people that have an open and understanding mind. When people connect with you through social media, some of them start to really feel like they know you. It can actually get a little dangerous. Facebook and Facebook inbox are two totally different beasts! On Facebook, everything is public. The Facebook inbox is private. You wouldn't believe some of the things that go on in that world.

You would not believe the type of pictures you may receive from bishop, pastor, or prophetess while they are sitting in the pulpit waiting to preach the word. Every bowed head checking his or her iPad is not reading the Bible and checking for scriptures. Their social media page exhibits the holiest of holy but their inbox is full of naked butts, penises, and breasts. They will send you their private parts that just went public to your inbox. Everyone is not who they appear to be.

When you are being followed on Twitter, when your pictures are looked at on Instagram, and you are connected with people through Facebook, people will begin to admire you. The dangerous part is that this is where admire becomes desire. People will, certainly not all; begin to want to be with you. I almost hate to make this statement, but I will. Many times when women, again certainly not all, come to my church that I have met on social media, they will appear to greatly enjoy the service. Notice, I said appear and you'll see why in a minute. Some will even join the ministry with undercover hopes of "us" hooking up. After being in the church for a few months and they begin to see that we aren't going to be getting jiggy with it, they leave! This causes people to start wondering what's going on and why is there such a high turnover rate with newly joined single women. I hate this with a passion. To be honest, I find myself not even opening the doors of the church unless my elders bring it to me as an issue. I hate it because it makes me look like I'm doing something to run them off, but actually I'm simply trying to be saved. I'm certainly not the only one that has this problem. There are a lot of others that have this problem as well and it is a mess to say the least.

If you don't give it up I'll spread a rumor

You'd be surprised at what some people will do when you turn them and their sexual offers down. You ever heard the statement that some people can't handle rejection? Well, it is so true. I wouldn't say which gender has it worse because I'm sure it's bad either way. I've heard of incidents in church when the pastor has turned down a sexual advance and that disgruntled member went coo coo for cocoa puffs! You see some people think that they are so fine or handsome and have such a great body that they will never in a million years be turned down. What they fail to realize is that they actually may be all that and a bag of chips, but some pastors are really saved and trying to do the right thing! Even if that leader has a weakness sexually for the opposite gender, there is a rule that most live by that goes like this, "Never crap where you eat!" This means he doesn't sleep with his own sheep. That is quite the truth. These turned down sex crazed members will make up vicious lies about their former pastor about why they left the ministry when in fact they left because they didn't get that leader in the sheets like they planned. Many have gone out telling lies such as I had to leave because pastor was hitting on me, I left that ministry because in the office the pastor made a pass at me, or pastor is a great speaker but I started getting uncomfortable when I was alone with him so I had to go! Some will outright say, "Pastor asked me to have sex with him and when I refused he stopped speaking to me." The sad thing about something like this is that some weak-minded person will actually believe this lie. The church's name is tarnished and the pastor has a bad reputation that can keep new members from joining especially if the hypocrite is spreading the lie faster than a forest fire. I know of pastors who were told face to face that if they didn't give it up, a rumor would be spread! I don't know about other pastors, but I refuse to let anybody blackmail this black male!

CHAPTER

I'M HOLY BUT STILL HORNY

A sex crazed church

Is it possible to be holy and yet horny? Some would say yes because getting horny is a human attribute just like being hungry, sleepy or thirsty.

Have you ever been to a church that had a bad reputation and was known to have a lot of players, gay people, or even swingers? Well, guess what? They exist and there are probably some in your town. These types of churches will have a high turnover rate. Some are mega churches and they have more than a thousand members. The turnover rate occurs because real saints leave when they discover this is not a real church, but a club disguised as a church. Say what you want, but the worst place you can be is in is a church that offers you a plane ticket to hell every Sunday. Sometimes, the church will be jam-packed leading you to believe there is a lot of God in the building. This is absolutely false. Haven't you heard the phrase, people draw people? That is true, even in churches. In churches like this, those that have a form of godliness, but deny the power thereof are right at home and comfortable. I, personally, know of one sex-crazed church where the pastor had to get up and make an announcement telling the gay men in the church to stop approaching the male visitors in a sexual manner because every man wasn't gay. He further explained that he was getting complaints from visitors. Among the heterosexuals, this is a player's paradise. This is a place where he can screw as many chicks as he wants under the same roof without the pastor ever reprimanding him for his behavior. He knows the pastor won't say anything to him because he is doing the same thing. This is a mess because now you have the women looking at each other sideways in service, while the man is laughing because none of them can claim him because he doesn't want a relationship, just fish and chips! Women in churches like this can sleep with married men without facing the consequences of their actions because this is acceptable at this church. I won't even mention all the gay people doing each other. We'll save that for another chapter.

Isn't it amazing that all of this can be going on and the pastor is ONLY preaching about God giving you a new home and putting a new car in your garage? These crooked pastors will never preach on holiness thus challenging the people to get their lives right because he or she is bumping and grinding too! I've personally counseled people who were connected to churches like this and they were some messed up people! It would blow your mind! I certainly don't claim perfection, but one thing I have witnessed and know is that when you find somebody that will play with God on that level, mental issues are not far behind. They usually turn into a crazy person and become extremely confused. The bottom line is sex sells and sex draws people that have that proclivity. Don't let that be you, my friend.

Singing and sexting

Did you know that Lucifer in the Bible was the praise leader in heaven? He was so awesome that the book of Ezekiel chapter 28 describes him as having beautiful stones such as topaz, sapphire, and diamonds covering his body! He literally had an organ and pipes built into his body. Needless to say, hell started in the music department. Have you ever noticed how the devil usually creeps into the music and singing department? If you ever want to know what spirit is in a church, check out the praise team! A church can have a very talented praise team that knows how to set the atmosphere in a church, but at the same time, it can be a very confused praise team under the music department. Many people that are living the gay lifestyle will be found working in this department. When you have a lot of gays or bold fornicators working in this department, you will attract all kinds of spirits that will eventually cause havoc in a church. You must understand that demonic spirits go where they can roam free and attract others. When somebody that is lascivious or gay freely operates over God's people, you can trust and believe they will bring all of these spirits to your church. These spirits will certainly attract other spirits and soon you'll find the church packed out! That is a subject we will explore later.

Today, church has moved into a technology age. This high-tech culture heavily uses texting and cell phones. People are now using their cell phones to read their scriptures in church while they follow the preacher. At the same time, the devil will use these devices for his purposes. People will sit in church and check their Twitter and Facebook accounts. It is crazy because while they are sitting in the congregation, you don't really know what they are doing. Some will even have the audacity to text others in the same congregation setting up their shenanigans for after service! Yes, I said it! They will text or shall I say "sext" right before your eyes and you have no idea what is going on. After praise and worship, they'll sit in the pulpit acting like they are reading their Bible app. Actually, they are setting up a love connection or shall I say a sex connection for later on that night, after revival. That devil is a smart fellow. He will use technology for the advancement of his tactics. Televisions, cell phones, computers, and iPads are great technology tools, but at the end of the night, the question is what are you using them for?

Married but still looking

Today, it is hard to believe that there are married church folks looking for somebody other than their spouse to sleep with. You have to wake up and realize that swingers are not just in the clubs, but also in some churches. Please understand that I am certainly not talking about all couples in church. How a man can watch another man have sex with his wife is nuts to me! Swinging started back in the college days when people were experimenting and trying new things. Let me throw this out there. Men may say they love ménage a trois, but trust and believe, it is usually never with their wife or a woman they are really interested in but with a woman they are just kicking it with. Listen to me clearly! Very few men would offer their wives to be in the mix of a threesome. If a man asks you to do a threesome, you better watch out! As the old folks would say, something in the water ain't clean! Usually that man has no real future aspirations for you.

Let's get back to the married, but still looking topic. Married, but not satisfied individuals may not be swinging but they can be looking for love in other places. They have a ring on their finger and they appear to be happily in love, but all along they are not. They are miserable, but for some reason they won't get a divorce. I have never understood that philosophy. These married but still looking people will paint their wives to be a witch spelled with a 'b' and make their husbands out to be worse than a bipolar patient. This causes you to look at their spouses crazy in church. Never forget that you are only hearing one side of the story. They have to paint their companion in this manner to get you to feel sorry for them and look the other way when they fall into this type of sexual affair. Once I had a woman say, she doesn't treat her husband right, so God has me in his life so he can still feel like a man. He told me she's his wife but I'm his soul mate! What? I told that sister she sounded like she had been smoking crack! How are you going to be his soul mate when he is already married with children? When the spirit of lust is on a person, they will say some of the craziest things.

When these cheaters pick up a dude or chick on the side, they won't be upfront and tell the person they don't plan on divorcing and just want some side action. There are so many sex and love starved folks in the church that they will find someone to accept their offer. Crazy as it sounds, I've known women that only get involved with married men! Isn't that a shame? Some women want what is already taken. I think this kind of woman looks at it as a challenge, not on the behalf of the wife, but on behalf of themselves to see if they still got it. Got what you ask? They want to know if they have the ability to take what is already taken. Who would want to possess that ability, especially when it comes to someone else's companion? Somebody with a sex-crazed spirit would possess this ability. To all those who are married but still looking or looking at who's already married, remember what goes around comes around. Let me be biblically correct:

> *"Whatsoever a man soweth that shall he also reap."*
> *Galatians 6:7 KJV*

Sending sex messages while preaching

The average church attendee will easily miss this one every time. This would be the least expected time you would expect to hear a preacher trying to send a message to a crowd of saints or even a specific person. What is actually happening right before your eyes and ears, is that the preacher speaking is throwing out hints of things they like romantically and even sexually. Let me just get down to it. Have you ever heard one of the following statements coming from a preacher in the pulpit?

- I've always been attracted to light skinned women.
- I love a sister with a little meat on her bones.
- Women with long hair are so attractive and it's an immediate turn on to me.
- There's something about a clean-shaven bald headed man.
- When I see a man with bowlegs, it does something to me.
- A man that takes care of his body, especially a muscular build, can get my attention any day.

This may not sound like much, but to any seasoned pastor or preacher, we know not to say what we like personally because it turns some on while it turns others off. When you are preaching, you are not filling out an application for an online Christian dating site. You should never go on and on about what you like about the opposite sex. How do you think a full-figured woman would feel about what you just said? How do you think a sister with a short, yet classy hairstyle or a woman that is very thin would feel? You have unconsciously made them feel like they are unwanted or unattractive without realizing it. I know you are saying that it may not be his intention and you are correct, but women can get easily offended when you start pointing out certain looks that they do not possess. I'm a single pastor and I had to learn this the hard way because I used to think nothing was wrong with it. Boy was I dead wrong.

Let's go deeper about the subliminal sex messages that are sent while preaching. I heard one female preacher say in the pulpit, "I was doing good serving God and abstaining from sex for seven years and then I slipped up. The bad thing about it, church, was it wasn't even worth it. The man was so small that by the time I realized he was in, he was done! He was little and had no stamina. If I'm going to fall, the man has to be packing and have the stamina of a bull because I can go all night!" What the hell! That is exactly what I'm trying to teach you guys. All she was doing was letting the players in the congregation know that I like well-endowed men that can go all night. Look at your face! I think you realize what I'm saying now, don't you? I heard one preacher say, "I got big feet and although I'm not from Texas, everything over here is big and I'm certainly not a member of the itty bitty committee!" That is reverend baller shot caller. He was sending out a message to the sex-crazed hoochies in the congregation that he was packing like a mandingo.

These are all examples of sex messages while preaching. Now that I told you, your ears will know it when you hear it. I can go on and on for days giving you different examples of these kinds of illicit messages, but I'll stop right here. It's sad to know that there are preachers who use their position to pick up men or women in God's house. If a single minister is asking a church attendee to go out on a date it is perfectly legal, but to send a sex message while preaching is ludicrous. You have to be one thirsty sister or brother to use the opportunity of spreading the gospel to pick up a freak in church. I can clearly see the old school saints say, "Child everybody behind the pulpit ain't preaching."

Don't wear that in the pulpit

A person once said, "You are what you wear." The pastor or preacher in the pulpit has all eyes on them for a certain period of time in a service. Everyone is looking at them holding on to the words that are coming out of their mouth. People are not only hearing, but as humans they are seeing. One of the worst things you can see in the pulpit is preachers whose outfits have taken everything away from their sermon. Have you ever seen a preacher with cutoff sleeves on his robe or the robe is so tight you can see every single body part clearly? I have and it's a mess to say the least. Why wear a suit or a dress so tight that women can see the imprint of your penis or men can see if you are wearing thongs or boy shorts? Yes, I said it. Whose attention do you really think this type of preacher is trying to get, God or a freak in the sheets? Oh, I mean in the pews! I've seen women preachers get up to preach and instead of saying amen you want to say got milk! I've seen with my own eyes some women preach in pants so tight that if you weren't prayed up you'd start throwing money at them like a stripper on a pole! Girl, don't you know all these brothers in the church aren't saved? Maybe that's why the altar is so packed after the sermon. They want you to lay hands on them, and on the way down they can sneak a squeeze of that basketball behind you. I've also witnessed gay male preachers preach in tight pants. All of this is happening in churches right around you and you know I'm telling the truth! I know you are trying to judge me, but it's all good. I'm just writing in a book what you talk about at the restaurant after church.

The church with no dress code. Shaking and shouting!

Dancing in the spirit, praising God, and giving Him what He deserves are all colloquialisms for shouting in the Spirit. This is a good thing especially when we reflect on all the things He has done for us. But the scripture says in 1 Corinthians 14:40 to let all things be done decently and in order. I am one who believes in the cliché— you can't clean the fish until you catch him. This simply means don't try to change a person until they are willing to change themselves. At the same time, remember when you are truly doing something for God it will be done right. I've seen people come to church to, supposedly, give God praise but it looks like they are dressed to hit the club or at least get attention. And I'm not talking about God's attention. Some people will wear something so provocative that you know God is the last one on their agenda. There have been instances in which some women danced so hard that their titties have literally popped out of their bra. Excuse me! While supposedly dancing in the spirit, they bend over and you can see the color of their thong! It's not about people looking, but if you are in front of the church you know that you will be seen. Have you ever seen a woman dancing, supposedly, in the spirit and she is shaking her booty like she is on a pole at Magic City? That is what I call shaking and shouting. Girl, please! You know good and well that is not for God. Tell me why when some people shout they have to come from the back of the church to the front trying to get everybody's attention? If you're really going to praise God, you won't be trying to turn the opposite sex on at the same time. All of these are signs that you have sex in the pews. Next time you hit the dance floor, I mean the altar, make sure you are giving it up to God and not somebody in the pews.

Why are preachers so horny after they preach? (Only preachers will understand)

This is a point that I really didn't want to explore because

I know many wouldn't understand. This is why I specifically shouted out the preachers. When you are high in the spirit and God is using you greatly, it is one of the best feelings a human being can experience. God speaking through you to sing or preach is amazing. It surpasses the feelings you get when on drugs, drunk, or even sex. Yet, something amazing happens almost immediately. Now, this statement comes from dozens of preachers I have interviewed and even myself, without me being afraid to say it. This is a very intriguing topic. You initially think how can God use you so greatly, yet you feel so fleshly after church. I'm not saying a person dives in the bed with someone they're not married to, but certainly after church the flesh needs to be put on lockdown. Many ministers have said to me, personally in conversation, that they feel extremely vulnerable. This is the kicker! Guess what? The devil himself knows ministers are extremely vulnerable at this time, so he sends everything at them.

When I first started ministering, I didn't understand why preachers would retreat back to the hotel or their homes right after service, but I do now. The best asset a preacher can have today is an armor bearer that has their back. That armor bearer keeps women from busting in the office, crowding around their car, or even asking for a personal conversation. The devil is a master at getting to the weak side of ministers at their weakest times. If you don't believe me, ask a preacher about this and they will agree even if they are a little reluctant. I'm not saying every preacher has these issues, but certainly most. I've had preachers tell me that they dip out quickly after church because church groupies will follow the deacon's car that is taking them to the hotel just to find out where they are staying.

After a preacher completes his time of ministering, he or she experiences a euphoric high that elevates him or her to a supernatural height. Your spirit ascends to a place that brings great satisfaction and blissful enjoyment. After preachers have completed their assignment, there is now a war in the soul and flesh and an unusual desire to experience a climax and reach a peak similar to the prior spiritual euphoric high. Many times, the soul and spirit is left wanting, therefore the desire for a climax intensifies. At that point, horniness is inevitable and the fervent craving to reach a peak becomes quite extreme. Horniness is a lustful arousal and sexual excitement. Preaching is typically an exciting time for a preacher. The spirit man is excited, the soul stimulated, and after the conclusion of a successful ministry assignment, the preacher's flesh can get out of control and he can't contain the excitement that he or she has just spiritually encountered. Horniness, now, becomes the avenue of expression that provokes a release of the feelings captured through stimulation. The flesh is excited, aroused, stimulated and ready for climax, orgasm, and passionate pleasurable release. During this kind of battle, the worst people you can be around are church freaks!

I could go much deeper into this, but I know you are already thinking I'm tripping. What I will say to the preacher is be sure to check yourself before you quickly wreck yourself after a service.

CHAPTER

THE GAY AGENDA IN THE CHURCH

You're either with us or against us

You really don't need me to convince you that there is a strong gay agenda going down in the house of God. There was a time you didn't hear about a gay movement in church, but today it's like the Wild Wild West! Let me clear up something before I continue. I'm not trying to get into any debate with this subject, nor do I believe in gay bashing. I simply believe what the Bible says. God created man to live a heterosexual life and have a heterosexual marriage. No debate and no argument out of me. I'll go on further to say that God loves all people and so do I. We should never degrade a person for their flaws. The Bible says:

> *"All have sinned, and come short of the glory of God." Romans 3:2 KJV*

The problem we have is that there is a big gay agenda going down in the house of God. Some of the most talented people in church today are living the gay lifestyle. From the musicians to the preachers, and do I even need to bring up the singers. The gay lifestyle is rampant in the church. There seems to be some type of takeover. Gay preachers have open, as well as, undercover movements going on in churches similar to a mob or gang. The gay community in church has some type of underground private club where ideas and concepts are exchanged almost guaranteeing your ministry to be successful, in the eyes of man that is. They will connect you with the best singers and musicians and they will get you grants from the government for your ministry, but you must have the same gay agenda. When they hold their major conferences around the country, they only use their own gay friends and the only way you get to preach on that platform is if you are gay. I feel the need to say this. I'm not saying every gay pastor or preacher is like this, but certainly some. There are some gay pastors struggling in their flesh to live a heterosexual lifestyle and they do not hang around gays for that very reason. To those brethren, I certainly applaud their efforts.

I'm not ashamed to admit that I use to have a big problem with gays and out of ignorance didn't show the love of God like I should have. The Lord dealt with me and changed my heart greatly. I will never have that spirit again and, sadly, a lot of church people possess this spirit. They can screw as many people of the opposite gender without being married, then have the nerve to down somebody that is gay! You have to be kidding! In the eyes of God, sin is sin. I recall a time when I was out having dinner with a group of preachers. The discussion was about how bad churches have become with open homosexuals and lesbians. One bishop said that every time a gay person comes into his church, he changes his sermon and preaches on that spirit. He really appeared to be homophobic and downright hateful towards gays. I stood out like a sore thumb saying how wrong that was to attack an individual and change your entire sermon simply because one walks in the service. I asked him if he changes his sermon when an adulterer, liar, or thief walks in. They all ganged up on me and said I'm too lenient towards gay people. I responded I'm lenient towards sinners like God was merciful towards me. Let me add that the majority of them were married and had hoes on the side. Their churches are known for sex related sins, but amongst heterosexuals. God help these pastors!

This gay agenda is something special because they will tell you that you are either with us or against us. That is totally not right because we simply don't believe the same. I'm against this gay agenda that many people participate in secretly, yet publicly try to state something else. One thing a preacher must have in today's society is the spirit of discernment. Without this, you will be fooled and tricked and may even be sucked into this agenda and don't even know it. At one time I was told, man if you were down with us your ministry would blow up! You would be on television, radio and be a household name! My response was, "If God don't do it, it won't be done. This brother doesn't swing from them vines!" All I know is birds of a feather certainly flock together. So glad I'm an eagle and don't mind soaring alone if I have to. Are you?

Living on the DL in the church

The club continues. This is a group of gay people who publicly act like they are straight when in fact they are not. The sad part is that the majority of them are married. I feel so sorry for their husbands and wives. Many of them know that if they ever came out of the closet, they stand to lose their churches and families. For this reason, they choose to live on the down low (DL) in the church. One of the greatest clues is that they constantly preach against the gay lifestyle. Aren't there any other sins that are plaguing our church and society? They preach like that because they don't want you to ever think that they are that way themselves. It's called, in my dictionary, spiritual homophobic behavior. This is such a dead giveaway! Do you think their spouses really don't know what is going on? Do you really think she doesn't see his feminine tendencies? Do you think that man doesn't see that "boy" spirit on her girlfriend who she says is just a cool friend and not her secret lover? Some people are not as stupid as you think they are. At the same time the Bible is so true when it says in 1 Peter 4:8 that love covers the multitudes of sins. This means that when you love a person, your love for them can, at times, cover the mess they are in.

Have you ever seen two people in a relationship and the other person was abusive physically and verbally, yet the abused person stays in that relationship? Have you heard a mother tell her daughter to get away from that no good man, but she doesn't budge? That is because love is covering an individual's wrong. I believe this frequently happens to husbands and wives that are married to somebody that is gay. Also, there are some people that look at their spouse's weakness as a small flaw in their character that is no different than a nicotine or alcohol habit. That is the furthest from the truth. Hopefully, they will see it for themselves. At the end of the day, we must pray for those living on the DL and their spouses. A lot of wives get a HIV diagnosis this way. Man, be straight up with your wife! Wife, be straight up with your husband. Even a liar wants to be told the truth.

Can gays really be delivered? Do you know of any?

We all know some people that are gay and they say they were born that way. I'm not going to get in a theological debate because David did say in *Psalms 51:5, "Behold, I was shapen in iniquity: and in sin did my mother conceive me."* He was telling us that he has been jacked up since birth. When a baby is in the womb, any spirit can connect to them. You can be born with a lying spirit, killing spirit, fighting spirit, then why not a gay spirit? I have seen this spirit in young men that are not even old enough to form the thought of sex! I've seen young boys three and four years old walking and talking like a little girl and you know I'm telling the truth. How is this so? Is it possible that a spirit entered in while they were in the womb or immediately after conception? This spirit appears to have such a stronghold hold on those that are gay. So many act like they cannot break free from it. I've had gay dudes say they were born this way and have NEVER been attracted to a woman. Wow!

Many individuals that I know that live the gay lifestyle seem to struggle greatly in their quest for deliverance. Some have gone as far as telling me they got married in hopes of killing their desire for men, but eventually the marriage ended in divorce and they went back to that lifestyle. You may not agree with this, but I applaud homosexual men that will set the unsuspecting wife free and not live a lie. To jack up somebody else's life and all along you don't even want her is deplorable. Let me ask you, do you know of any men that used to be gay and are totally straight now? Many have even defiantly said, "I was born this way and I will die this way!" My God. Some will tell you not to waste your time praying for deliverance because God made them the way they are. When I hear talk like this, it sometimes makes me speechless.

I was talking with a preacher friend of mine who used to be gay and he said that when he reveals his past in a new blossoming relationship, the woman cuts him off and aborts the relationship. Why is it men have no problem dating a former lesbian, but women don't want to date a former homosexual? Isn't gay, gay? Are people then saying once gay always gay? Does that mean God doesn't have the power to totally deliver? Let me go further. If a person used to be gay and is now delivered, do you think that they should tell the person they are dating? This is a very touchy subject and very few people can handle it. To that extent everybody can't handle your past or your testimony. This is a real life situation and it is more common than you think. It takes not only spirituality, but also common sense. Think about it!

The question that must be raised is —is there any sin that God cannot deliver man from? According to the word of God, the answer is a simple no. The redemptive power of Christ can reach way down into the tunnels of sin and redeem anybody. The Bible clearly says:

> "Therefore if any man be in Christ, he is a new creature: old things are passed away; behold, all things have become new." 2 Corinthians 5:17 KJV

God's power through Jesus can deliver a homosexual or lesbian, if they truly desire to be delivered. One thing we all know about God is He doesn't force deliverance on anyone that doesn't want it. It doesn't matter how long a person has been gay or even if they believe they were born that way, God can and will deliver if they want to be delivered! Homosexual, bisexual, transsexual, lesbian or whatever it is, Satan's power is nowhere near as strong as God's power! My brothers and sisters, never feel you are out of the reach of His power. I get such great joy when I hear of a person that was bound by homosexuality or any sin and they are fully delivered witnessing to others of his grace, power, and mercy!

Who you traveling with playa...I mean preacha?

Birds of a feather will fly and flock together. It may sound old, but it sure is the truth. When ministers go on the road traveling conducting revivals and conferences, they usually take a few people with them and nothing is wrong with that. Sometimes, we have a big mess. Often times you will have gay pastors that travel all over the world with very young men who are "homosexuals in training." The gay older man will get the young, innocent, and most of the time, feminine young man and pay them to be their so called armor bearer. Also, one of the newest names that are being used is "Godson." Now please remember that this is not always the case. Most of these young men are also struggling financially and in between odd jobs. There are usually no fathers around either because, trust and believe, pops would pick up on what is happening a mile away!

Some of these young men emulate their pastor and really don't know they are being set up to be his permanent piece! Older man and young man, you didn't think that all cougars were just females did you? I did an intense study last year while pursuing my bachelor's degree. This dates way back to Africa thousands of years ago. Women would give their young sons to kings and men of great affluence from the age of about 10 to 18. They would literally become a sex servant to these men believing that they would be able to make them much stronger for life. After that time, the young men would be returned to their families and would live a heterosexual lifestyle. It is almost like history is repeating itself. This is public knowledge. To the young men that are unsuspecting, trapped, or are just in this lifestyle my prayers go out to you.

The gays ARE right!

There is a major point of view that the gay movement has made that really has me thinking and praying. Many of them say they know they are in sin, but why do so many preachers preach against them in hatred and not in love? If the same preacher preaches on fornication or adultery and he or she preaches that in love, what is the major difference? If sin is sin, aren't they both in the wrong? Guess what? Whether you like it or not, they are 100 percent correct. Again, this is the second time I'm quoting this scripture:

> "The Lord hath appeared of old unto me, saying, Yea, I have loved thee with an everlasting love: therefore with lovingkindness have I drawn thee."
> Jeremiah 31:3 KJV

If we showed all sinners love, regardless of their weakness or issues, I truly believe the church would be just as packed as the nightclubs. You may not agree, but right is right and wrong is wrong. I have heard gay people being called all types of words from the pulpit by a preacher that is bent on sending them straight to hell. In the exact same sanctuary, you have those that lie, steal, cheat, talk about one another, men having sex with women they are not married to and vice versa and this same preacher is silence of the lambs on all the other sins. Something is wrong with that messenger in the pulpit.

Let me give you an inside scoop; just don't tell anybody I told you! Most times when you hear of a preacher slamming down and preaching predominately on one particular sin, in this case homosexuality, usually he or she is trying to cover themselves, so people will never accuse them of that sin. That is what you call a sanctified smoke screen!

Chapter

BABY OIL OR HOLY OIL?

People that come to church with the wrong agenda

There is not a church on the globe that can avoid this type of problem. Regardless of the denomination or affiliation, people will come with or without your approval. The tricky thing about this is the average pastor wants a packed house. The question he or she must ask is—what is this church packed with? It is very easy to pull the young crowd, the professional, the money, and even the gay crowd. Individuals will come to church for the wrong reasons. In the 21st century, the average leader will encounter sheep as well as goats, but it will take a spiritual eye to know the difference. Some will be sent by God to bless the ministry financially and will even involve themselves in every way to see that ministry get off the ground and stay off the ground. Concurrently people will be sent to certain ministries by the devil, wearing disguises that look like they were made up for a Hollywood horror movie. One pastor told me about an incident that took place after he had prayed for years to have a church mother. On a sunny Sunday morning, a new "church mother" comes to church dressed in all white from her head to her feet. She joined his church that morning and began to work faithfully with him. The membership grew and the young women began to flock to her as a chicken to a hen. After a while, he noticed that the mother began to have great influence over the women in the church. It was more than he did! She began holding services in her house at the same time as his services. Moved by the Spirit, one day, he ended his service very quickly and went to her house. Something told him to go look in the window and what he saw caused his jaw to drop! All the women were laid out naked while the mother was putting "holy" oil on them. Would you believe that they were speaking in other tongues, not unknown tongues? What a mockery of spiritual influence over innocent sheep. This was no Mother in Zion, but a Mother Hubbard. That pastor immediately disfellowshipped that so-called mother and warned all saints to stay away from her. It is sad to say that only half of the women recovered and came back to the ministry. You've heard the proverb that everything that is shiny is not gold. Don't think for one minute that everyone that comes to join the ministry comes to build it up! There are wolves in sheep clothing that come to tear your house down.

Preachers who pursue the saints

Power and influence is attractive to people! This can be a lure for members. There are some pastors, bishops and preachers that use their title and position to get whatever they want from the opposite gender. Why would you say no to God's mouthpiece that you see being used every Sunday? Preachers have a way of noticing the desperate, lonely, and thirsty congregants. There are those that will do whatever they say simply because of their position over them. They will begin to show that member special attention or preferential treatment. They will tell that member that he or she is unique and a gift from God. Remember, most preachers are the smoothest when it comes to words, phrases and telling people exactly what they want to hear at the right time.

Communication is one of a preacher's greatest strengths. Conversation can start with a simple text message then escalate to late conversations. Eventually, texting or shall I say, sexting after midnight which involves pictures will begin to occur. Need I say more because you know where this is going? Next, they are off to the hotel to get mo-tail! Yes, there are preachers, male and female, that will go after every good-looking member that is in their church because they are simply off the hook. Do you know what the perfect remedy is for this type of situation? Don't join a church like that and pray for the preacher instead of talking about him! Remember, the Good Book says in *Psalm 105:15 KJV,* *"Saying, Touch not mine anointed and do my prophets no harm."* I know that is hard for many of you to do because you'd rather go to the National Enquirer-Church Edition with pictures, receipts, and facts to spread vicious and slanderous comments that will topple that ministry and pastor. Well, my friend, you have just fallen into one of the oldest traps in Christendom. You have just given them free publicity! You have officially created the HYPE that just HELPED the preacher go HIGHER. Out of your persecution comes his promotion. Don't shoot the messenger!

Saints who pursue the preacher

Whatever you do, don't get it twisted because the preachers are not the only pursuers. There are saints sitting on sexy pews, rubbing their hands, and licking their lips waiting for the right moment to tap that. God help if that preacher is handsome or beautiful and can preach. It's mighty hard to preach when you are being looked at with eager eyes and wet lips! Oh and don't let them be blessed with the ability to dress. A fine Armani suit, sleek Red Bottom Louboutins and a stellar custom tailor made ensemble will make it worse. The gate has just been opened! I've learned one thing when I hear about a minister and a member getting jiggy with it! I do not jump to conclusions and think it's the minister's doing because it could be the member. I have been to ministries where the loose women in the church had an inside bet on who can get the preacher in bed before the revival was over. They would come up to him or her teary eyed and broken asking for extra prayer and counseling. All of this was just a spiritual set up for a sexual cum up! Wow!

Hoes in the house (male and female)

What classifies someone as a hoe? Most would say a hoe is a person that sleeps with multiple people at the same time without getting caught. Please don't let the word hoe offend you especially if you're not one. Hoes are not only at the basketball games, malls, and restaurants. Hoes are everywhere! In this case, they are particularly at the church. Some come to get delivered, while others come to select their next victim. As a man, I believed most hoes were men, but today the title seems to fit women too. What a double standard! Just like the woman in the Bible who was caught in adultery, everyone automatically assumes it was her that was married, but guess what it could have been him! All we know is one of the two were married. But isn't it amazing that Jesus never tried to find out who was the adulterer but rather said in *John 8:7 KJV, "He that is without sin among you, let him first cast a stone at her."* I flipped the script to let you see that it could be possible that hoes are in the house to be changed. Male hoes are who they are because they've never experienced true love. Female hoes are who they are because this lifestyle is now their way of getting back in a revengeful way at men that have used them. The challenge is if there is sex in the pews, instead of Christian love, the hoe will remain a hoe instead of a whole individual again. Let's learn to be merciful towards people who only feel connected in life by a physical climactic touch instead of a spiritual touch.

Remember Rahab in the Bible. She was a hoe, but after encountering holy men for a short time she got delivered and never lived that lifestyle again (Joshua 6:17). A red cord hanging out of the window saved her. The red cord represents the Blood. The Blood of Jesus has the power to change anyone from anything. As a matter of fact she is the great (almost times 10) grandmother of Jesus Christ! What can you say about that? Hoes can change! If many of us would be honest, we would say amen, but I forgot let's keep your deliverance on the DL (down low).

Stop burning that strange fire!

All kinds of fires are being burned in our churches today. In the Bible, burning fires was a means the people would use to get God's attention or to simply worship and sacrifice. The Hebrew word translated "strange" means unauthorized, foreign or profane. Many people in church have different strengths. Some people are anointed by God to do the right thing while others are anointed by the devil to wreak havoc on the body of Christ. You are anointed by God to do the right thing, but you can also be anointed by the devil to do wrong things. All oil is not holy oil. Do you have holy oil or just baby oil? It's about to get hot and heavy, so if you can't hang, this is a good time to go to the next chapter!

During the days of Moses, people were creating fake anointings and burning strange fire!

> "And Nadab and Abihu, the sons of Aaron, took either of them his censer, and put fire therein, and put incense thereon, and offered strange fire before the LORD, which he commanded them not."
> Leviticus 10:1 KJV

These guys were giving and doing what they wanted and not what God commanded them to do. This is what made it strange fire.

In church, there are ministers using any and all types of gimmicks to get the pews filled. Some preachers are drawing people to their ministries based on their physical looks, but can't preach their way out of a paper bag with holes in it! Women will follow a good-looking, non-anointed man just like men will follow a good-looking non-anointed woman. You'd be surprised at what a smooth shaved, long silky weave, or well-toned body will do for some pastors. Some leaders have charisma (which is the Greek word for gift) and they use it to greatly manipulate followers. They are great smooth talkers that have the gift of gab but never quote one scripture in a whole sermon! There's nothing wrong with being a good talker, but when you're talking simply to get somebody naked or their money, then Houston we have a problem! Some have great popularity because they were formally an actor or athlete, so people are mesmerized by who they are instead of the word of God they bring. Others have great influence because they are rich! People tend to follow 'prosperity' ministries in hopes of becoming rich. That is not true in its entirety. Every good-looking or affluent leader doesn't use his or her looks and wealth negatively, but a great deal do and you know I'm telling the truth. There's a whole lot of strange fire being burned in churches on Sunday morning, so beware. The Bible speaks strongly against it.

> *"Even as Sodom and Gomorrah, and the cities about them in like manner, giving themselves over to fornication, and going after strange flesh, are set forth for an example, suffering the vengeance of eternal life." Jude 1:7 KJV*

When you burn strange fire, you will always draw strange flesh! Sadly, that is their oil or shall I say fire.

I'm in love with my pastor! Should I find another church?

I'm sure you have heard of this and it is far too common. Pastors, male and female, all have members who desire to be with them and not in a hallelujah way! The ability to counsel and teach people how to overcome their problems can give a pastor a hero complex. I counseled a young man that was in love with his female pastor to the point that he obsessed about her even during her sermons on Sunday morning! He would almost literally be drooling at the mouth sitting in the pews as she preached! He asked me if it would be best for him to leave his church and find another. What do you think? The role of a pastor does attract many, but some are able to keep their feelings to themselves or not have them at all. Would it be better to join a church where you are not attracted to your leader? Depending on your level of attraction, it may be best for you to leave if you can no longer receive the message, but only want the messenger. Why go somewhere spiritual where your only reaction is carnal? I stated in my first book LAPD (Life After a Painful Divorce) that sometimes admire could lead to desire. When saints constantly look at their pastor as someone they admire, if they are not careful, they will soon begin to desire him or her. The trivial thing about it is the unsuspecting pastor sometimes has no idea what is going on. I've heard of stories of members leaving a church because they cannot control their inward feelings towards their leader. Instead of sitting in Sunday morning service receiving a word from heaven, they are receiving hot thoughts from hell. Yes, it is time to go. Nothing should hinder hearing the word of God. Not even you!

Of course, everyone doesn't have this problem, so please hear my heart. There are some people that can see their pastor as their spiritual guide only. Has this ever happened to you or someone you know? I can almost guarantee you that many members have fallen into this pitfall. The sad thing is the pastor usually is characterized as bad when in actuality it's the distorted mind of a member who can't contain and refrain. Is it the pastor's fault? How can it be? This is comparable to every actor or actress that has a stalker following him or her. Is it appropriate to say he or she acted too well in their last movie? If people could only receive the message from the messenger, then we all could get along.

The single pastor (male and female)

Who said the pastor had to be married? I hear that quite often, but there is no scripture that speaks of such recommendation. As a matter of fact, out of the twelve disciples that Jesus hand selected, we only hear about one of them being married which was Peter. On occasion the Bible talks about Jesus healing Peter's mother from a fever (*Matthew 8:14 KJV*). Being a single pastor is a big challenge. This type of leader, fortunately and unfortunately, will have people join the ministry thinking that they are the missing link. You can't tell them that God didn't give them a dream telling them that the pastor is their husband or wife. It is absolutely crazy and ridiculous. They really believe that just because they say the dream came from God, the pastor is supposed to acquiesce to their request. One pastor told me that he hears he is someone's husband from different females in his congregation so often that he no longer gets mad and tells them off. He said he says if it is of

God, I'll see you at the wedding, sweetheart. His method is not to fight it but to let it be. Of course, it turns out to be nothing at all. By the way, I'm talking about me. Often times, pastors receive a lot of gifts and financial contributions because members try to be a blessing to him or her out of their flesh and not of the spirit. The sad thing about this is that there are so many single pastors who want to marry, but unfortunately they are in a sea of thirsty sharks that want them. They're not wanted for who they are as a person, but for their position in the Kingdom. Who wants a man or woman that only wants you because you are a pastor? Love should have nothing to do with what a person does for a living, but rather who they are as a person. How do you know so well you ask? Because I am fortunately and unfortunately a single pastor. I hope you're praying for a brother.

I have a pastor friend of mine on the West Coast who says a woman in church pursued him for over three years. He finally caved in to her sexual demands. This occurred during a time when his current relationship was having issues. Actually, she had gone on a sexual strike and hadn't given it up in over three months! That is a whole different story. Anyway, when he gets to her house, it smelled like candied apples with a touch of butter. He said the sheets were like none he'd ever felt before. She was looking more beautiful than she had looked at church. Luther was playing in the background with two glasses of wine on the bed stand. He said the ambiance was so perfect that it looked like a page in Satan's weekly sex magazine! Filled with lust and desire, they passionately kissed and he says he clearly remembered her lips tasting like cinnamon. Everything was so right, but in his spirit, he still felt wrong. She began to take off his Timberlands and Levi jeans along with his wife-beater. He obliged and removed a silky red lingerie set that she had to have gotten from Victoria. In his mind, he was saying "I lasted so long against her attempts for over three years and she finally got to me and here I am laying on her California King size bed!" After reaching for the Magnum in his pants pocket, he turned around and as he looked in her eyes they became big and glossy almost like an animal! He said she began to laugh and laugh in an uncontrollable and extremely loud manner. It began to sound like ten women were in the room as the laughs filled the room like a surround sound movie! He began to call her name and ask her what was wrong, but it was like she didn't or maybe couldn't hear him because of the volume of the laughs. He said it was like something took over her body. After 60 seconds, which seemed like an hour of her jerking and laughing uncontrollably, he grabbed his clothes and jetted out of the room! When he got to the driveway to get in his truck, he could still hear her laughing! Crazy!

At church the following Sunday, he calls her to the side to see what the heck was her problem and to ask if she was all right. She looked at him like he was joking and said, "Why you playing? You were never at my house!" What the hell! I wish I did make this up. You should hear him tell this story. It's almost like you can literally feel the story in your spirit! The devil is nothing to play with it, whether you choose to believe me or not. All pastors, male and female, most likely have people in their church that have voluntarily signed up with the devil to get you to fall. Stand strong soldiers! You can pass the test. With a spirit like that, imagine the kind of spell the pastor could be put under? Saints in the pews, never stop praying for your pastor. The devil knows if he can get to the head, the body doesn't stand a ghost of a chance.

It is easy to look at your pastor like they are an all spirit being and that they are the leader and the voice that God uses to encourage and strengthen you. Don't forget they are flesh and blood too, which means they are not above making mistakes. You hear all the time about pastors falling from grace. Today we have so many young pastors that know it all, so mistakes are bound to happen. Inexperience and lack of wisdom is the reason for this problem. I know I'm repetitive on this and have said it a few times in this book, but don't ever think your pastor is so strong that they don't need your prayers. Imagine one man or woman praying for 100 or 200 members weekly yet they themselves only got 5 or 10 of their members praying for them! Doesn't that seem drastically unfair? A pastor can be the perfect target because there are only a few praying for him. If they fall from grace, it is actually the only way they will know who is on their side. He or she will know by who leaves and who stays. Let me take it even further and I hope you can handle this true analogy. What would you do if your pastor confessed to the congregation that they got someone pregnant or even they themselves are pregnant and they are single? Would you stay or leave? Would you forgive them? Would you leave and tell everybody you know how much of a hypocrite he or she is? This is real and happens all the time. You want to know what is the bitter truth about sexual incidents like this? Are you sure you can handle the truth? Okay, I believe you. They usually will go out of town, so they won't bump into their own members or Christians that may know them and get an abortion! We as leaders have to forgive you, but members have an extremely hard time forgiving us. And guess what? We all read from the same Bible! I know what you are saying. They should have known better. But shouldn't YOU have known better, too? What a double standard.

The single pastor constantly has to hear about how bad they need a husband or wife, especially, if they want the ministry to grow. There is not one single scripture that reinforces this theory. Of course, it will create a family structure to see in the forefront of the ministry. A family unit consists of a husband, wife and children. Yet, every ministry doesn't have that. As a matter of fact, I know many preachers that preach members in, while their mean wives run them out. Sorry you made me say that. Friends, family, and other members always have somebody that 'You just have to meet!' It's easy for them to select somebody they think fits your life, but what if it's not somebody you love? Personally, people are constantly trying to hook me up with a good singer or even a preacher that they feel will take my ministry to the next level. You know what? I asked myself after being divorced for eight years "Do I want a woman that is perfect for my profession or perfect for me? Does it really matter if she can take her voice down to the pit and back to the penthouse all in one note? Does it matter that she can preach like a popular TV evangelist? What if after the revival and conference is over we don't get along at the house? What if we are not personally compatible? If we can't be happy outside of church, what seems perfect in public can be a hot mess in private! The first case of leprosy in the Bible was when God smote Moses' sister Miriam with it because she came against his wife of another ethnicity.

> *And Miriam and Aaron spake against Moses because of the Ethiopian woman whom he had married: for he had married an Ethiopian woman. Numbers 12:1 KJV*

Do you notice how it mentions her race twice in one verse? You can clearly see God wasn't having it! In Moses' case, it was a racial thing, but in this day and age, it is usually social, educational, and even financial. Somebody once asked an unusual question to a popular single African American pastor on the East Coast. He was asked, "If you married a white woman do you think any of the eight hundred black women in your church would leave?" He refused to answer the question and he changed the subject saying that it wasn't important to discuss. What do you think especially if you are a single black woman? I forgot this is a book not a survey. If you don't want the pastor to pick your spouse, then you should let them pick his or her own as well.

CHAPTER

HURT IN THE HOUSE

When your companion cheats with someone in church

To have your spouse step out on you is a pain that is almost unbearable. This scenario is further complicated when it involves members of the same church! Church is supposed to be the place where angels are not demons, right? What do you do when you come to the place called church to be made whole again only to have to look up in the pulpit and the one leading worship is also the one leading another kind of worship with your companion? God help us all if the culprit is the preacher behind the mic that is supposed to be bringing you a word from the Lord to strengthen your soul! This is crazy to say the least, but it's happening at a church near you whether you believe it or not! Who do you run to when you thought you were running to God and wind up running dead smack into the devil, in God's house?

When you have to ask another Christian woman, would you please leave my husband alone—you will have hell up in the church. To take it a step further, what about when a pastor knows that a married person is cheating on his or her spouse and the two individuals wind up hooking up and getting married. If this preacher never said or did anything about it, that is one damned preacher! That is way out of order and he or she will certainly have to stand before God concerning how he is leading God's people. I know these situations are quite touchy, but somebody has to take a stand. This is my personal belief and stand in my ministry, but I'll say it just the same. You only talk to one woman or one man at a time per year in the church I pastor and being that I'm a single pastor that would include me! Imagine being in a church and one man dates four different women in the same church in the span of a year? You will have at least three women looking at each other crazy and most likely they won't be members of the church for long. That is too much attitude for one sanctuary!

I had a preacher friend in Kentucky tell me that he knew his wife was cheating when she started wanting to go to church every time the church doors were opened. You would automatically think that sounds like a good thing, right? You are dead wrong! Remember I told you that people come to church for all kinds of reasons. Well, this is one of those reasons. He continues to tell me that he had a clue who it was in the church, but this person's position was so big in the ministry that he had to be completely sure. He installed a wiretap on his phone line with the phone cord in the basement. He taped her for almost two days straight. What he heard almost sent him into a nervous breakdown! He heard the assistant pastor saying things to his wife like, "I know you going to let me hit that again tonight right? C'mon boo, you know you can't whip a brother like the other night and now leave me feening! Let's meet at the normal spot then drive around for a little to make sure you're not being followed. We can't take any chances! I love you!" Oh my God! He said he almost lost his natural born mind! He knew that preacher's voice a million miles away. But, with his wife? Never in a million years would he have believed this could happen, and happen to somebody like him. I would tell you how that story ended, but you probably wouldn't even believe me.

When a painful scenario occurs in the church, the problem is harder to overcome and the healing takes longer. Church is a place where you probably exchanged wedding vows, had your children christened, got delivered from strongholds, and learned your greatest lessons about faith in God. For that to happen, you almost feel like a terrorist and want to blow that church off the map! Almost instantly, the offended one feels mad and pissed off with everybody in the church, even though it was one or two people that offended them. For some reason, they feel like everybody knows and in most cases, the general public doesn't know at all. To have to come back in church when maybe a few know what happened is quite embarrassing. One of the saddest things about this, I experienced this first hand, is for people to hear about what has happened and instead of hugging you and pledging their support, they'll walk right around or past you like you got the swine flu! And we wonder why some people leave church and never ever come back! This could be one of the reasons.

I don't trust any of these Christians

If I had a dollar for every person who has made that statement, I'd be one wealthy fellow. Looking from the other side, I understand exactly what they are saying. To break it down for you, what they are really saying is we don't trust none of those people who act like they are Christians. Real Christians can be trusted; perhaps you just haven't met any yet. When a person wears the moniker of a Christian person, people think they are Christ-like. They should be, but sadly all of them are not. Maybe it's a term they are using by faith, in hopes of them one day being totally sold out for Christ. The worst thing you can do is to believe that a title exempts a person from injustices. I know some may not like this statement but I've met some of the best and most important people at church. Yet, at the same time, I've encountered some of the nastiest, stankiest, slickest, conniving, low down, and down low dirty shames right in church! They will smile in your face, yet talk behind your back! They will steal your wallet out of your purse as quick as they will steal your man or woman. You can't trust them with your business or it will be on Entertainment Tonight, Church Edition! This is the catch! I'm obviously not talking about everybody but certainly somebody! The bottom line is don't believe somebody because of his or her title or his or her proclamation claiming to be a Christian. Instead, let his or her conduct speak for itself.

An interview with lesbians

I was in a revival in the Washington DC area some years ago and after the service the pastor asked me to speak with two women in his church that had a very unique case. He said he trusted my judgment as a man of God and he felt led to have me deal with this case. These two women were married to each other. They said they believe nothing is wrong with their relationship and they love God and His Word. They were faithful members of this church and tithed regularly. They'd just purchased a $300,000 home in Maryland and the wife had a 5-carat ring on her wedding finger. They displayed such a warm, hospitable, and loving spirit. They began to explain that some of the members in the church didn't want them there saying they were a bad example of Christians. They never did anything bad, but because of the lifestyle they were living the saints didn't want them in their church. What should we do, preacher, they asked? They said they loved their church and their bishop, but they didn't know how much more of the abuse they could take at the hands of the members. I was in a very awkward position to say the least. I quickly started praying in my spirit while they were shedding tears telling me about the nasty things that were being done. I told them to continue to come to church and look past all of the things the saints were doing. They began to smile and cheer up. However, before we left the office, I told them that their lifestyle was not in accordance with the word of God. They have to really pray and ask God to give them deliverance. Their problem is greater because they feel no guilt after the sin. This complicates their problems. I told them when I was a weed smoker, cocaine snorter, and womanizer that I didn't feel bad about it, but that didn't make it right. When I smoked weed, I convinced myself that it was okay because weed comes from the earth and God created the earth, so what's wrong with that? What a fool I was. When I was chasing women I made myself believe that I was really helping them out by giving them the privilege of being with a real man. I always treated them like queens, so what's wrong with that? Little did I realize that it wasn't my duty to put a smile on every woman's face, but reserve it for the woman God gave solely to me. They began to slowly understand, although, they were being honest with me and realized they were in a conundrum.

What do you do when the Word says one thing, but your heart is saying something different? It's easy for many of you to say well just obey the word, but do you say that when it comes to your own life and decisions you've had to make? I've been preaching now over half of my life and if there is something I have realized about God is that he is unlike man because he's patient with us. One of my favorite verses in the entire Bible:

> "Is not my word like as a fire? Saith the Lord: and like a hammer that breaketh the rock in pieces."
> Jeremiah 23:29 KJV

The prophet was saying that some people have to sit under the Word. As they sit under the Word, it breaks up their hard heart of sin. Watch this and try to be honest with yourself, not me. Weren't there things you were doing that were not godly, but you were still coming to church? Yet, after sitting under a leader that saw the good in you and not just the bad, they continued to preach the gospel to you week after week believing God for your breakthrough. As a genuine man of God, my total confidence is never in social programs, but rather the pure word of God. I told them to stay right there in the church and keep coming on Sundays and Bible class. I just believe that the Word can and will change anybody from anything! Yes, that is my story and I'm sticking to it! I had to ask myself this question. Do we put heterosexuals out that are bumping and grinding with folks they are not married to? Do we ask the liars to leave? God said in His Word in Psalms 101:7 that a liar can't tarry in His sight. What about the person that is running everybody down or the one that doesn't give a dime to the house of God despite how God has blessed them? I think you got my point. No one should be put out of the church especially if they're trying to get themselves together. I am very leery of so-called preachers and pastors that will put people out of their churches that don't have their same proclivity. Please keep these leaders in prayer because the House of God is for everybody, especially those that are trying to get right.

How can you be saved and do this to me?

A person that has been redeemed by the blood of Jesus Christ and is now living the life of a saved individual would not fathom doing certain things. This chapter is dedicated to individuals that have had horrifying and embarrassing things done to them by the hands of saved people. If you read the Bible and you see what King David did to poor Uriah, you would be shocked that even God would call him a man after his own heart. David wanted his wife Bathsheba so bad that he had poor Uriah killed! Out of all the women he could have, he wanted another man's wife! That story is one of the worst things I personally have ever read in the Bible. Let's go further. A person can have a great character, but a situation can change your impression of him or her. Peter was a part of Jesus' inner circle, but he denied Jesus three times and on the third time, he cursed a little girl out! Yet, Peter delivered the sermon on the day of Pentecost. These stories exist in the Bible, but people are living these stories today in the church! During my twenty plus years of evangelizing I've encountered so many of my colleagues that either did or survived some of the worst events ever, even some of you.

SPIRITUAL SEXUAL HEALING

They don't represent God or the church

To anyone that was a victim of a so-called representative of God and the church, understand they indeed are not! They are not just sheep in wolves' clothes, but shepherds in wolves' clothes. My pastor taught me a lesson in the infant stages of my walk with Christ that I will never forget. He said don't ever think that some people can't be used by the devil because they can. Judas walked with Jesus for three and a half years. He saw Jesus raise Lazarus from the dead, heal Bartimeus from blindness, and even cast the devil out of a possessed boy yet Judas let Satan use him to betray Jesus. If a man can be with Jesus in the flesh and still side with the devil, what do you think about somebody who has never seen Him? One of my favorite scriptures in the Bible talks about this very thing. But I am not surprised! In 2 Corinthians 11:14 it says that even Satan disguises himself as an angel of light. Most of the titles that people have today are nothing more than a key that gives them access to unlock the hearts of people. You have to wake up and realize we are in the last days and the devil is using people to destroy others. I talked about this briefly in my first book LAPD (Life After a Painful Divorce). Many people in marriages and relationships have had their heart broken and vow never to love again simply because of what they endured by the hands of one person.

No one person should ever have that much power over us that we give up on love. A relationship that ends on bad terms shouldn't give a person a license to hate every one of the opposite gender. You shouldn't say like King Solomon, "I'm sick of love!" I've known people to get so mad at the opposite gender that they turned to their same gender and began living the gay lifestyle. That is too much! These vicious people are not God's representatives. They are fulfilling their own deviant sexual fantasies. I must say this and hopefully you won't get offended.

Everybody is NOT a victim and some people knew exactly what they were getting into. When you choose to sleep with a person, you must calculate other risks that are involved. I know women who get involved with married men and think he's going to leave his wife and when he doesn't, she flips out. Now come on, really? If you choose to get involved with anybody that is not yours, you must expect some collateral damage. Good girls like bad boys! Bad boys like good girls! Light attracts dark and vice versa. I can't tell you how many times I've counseled one of the young sister saints at the church about how she got played like XBox fooling up with a street cat. When you mess with dogs, you will catch fleas' period. When you are of age, you should have known better. Whether its street men or street women, they play on another level. The game is called "get them before they get you." Expect the following: your credit to get ruined, a black eye, and tickets on your car that you let them drive. Sorry, I don't give sympathy in some areas especially when I know you know better. I have three beautiful sisters and every time they had a baller shot caller in their lives that had more game than PlayStation, I told them clearly what was up. If they continued to fool with him, they knew they were playing at their own risk. If that person you get involved with is a bishop, pastor, prophetess or whoever, when the holy conscience hits them and they want to stop playing church and do right, your heart just might get left! Never play the role of a victim when you knew exactly what you were getting into. It is one thing to really be a victim and it is another thing to make yourself a victim.

Contrary to some, the church is full of good people that are sent from God to help you miss hell and make it to heaven. One of the most hateful expressions I have ever heard is, "I don't go to church because all those people in church are fake and no good!" That is a lie from the pit of hell. Yes, there are some fake people in church. But check this out, there are people at your jobs that are no good yet you get up and go to work five days a week. There are fake and no good people at Walmart yet you go there weekly to shop. You know why? You are not going to Walmart for the no-good and fake people, but instead for a product. It is the same principle when a person comes to church. We should be coming for Jesus and not the potential hypocrites that may be there. Remember, you have some no good fake relatives, but you are still a member of that family!

This is the part where most people won't understand and perhaps some will. You have great men and women of God that have fallen into sin and demonstrated characteristics that were not godly. Yet, if they repent God forgives them and they have an opportunity to be who God truly called them to be. Remember, there is no sin under the heavens besides blasphemy that God won't forgive you of; rape and molestation included. This is a hard and bitter pill to swallow because sometimes victims want revenge in many different ways. Know that no one gets away with offending God's children. As the old school used to say, "You might get by but you won't get away!" All through the scriptures you will find examples of God's men and women doing despicable things, but when they repented he forgave them of their sins. When I looked at how David killed a man because he wanted his wife, I was amazed. Yet when his conscience hit him he repented.

> *Have mercy upon me, O God, according to thy lovingkindness: according unto the multitude of thy tender mercies blot out my transgressions. Wash me thoroughly from mine iniquity, and cleanse me from my sin. For I acknowledge my transgressions: and my sin is ever before me. Psalms 51: 1-3 KJV*

Ask yourself, what else can a person do who was once wrong, and they are trying to get right?

Delivered from the attack of your enemy

I am convinced that nothing just happens. To the thinking

mind, it almost appears as if God stepped back and allowed certain bad things to happen to us. I know you may not think like this, but I certainly do. I sometimes am boggled by why God doesn't stop certain things from happening. Imagine yourself as a young boy at the tender age of seven years old at church with the choir director. The child thinks he is with the director more than the others because he is special when in fact he is the next unsuspecting victim of an rapist. The choir director corners him off in the church basement and no one is around to hear the child scream. Now, ravished and confused the young boy is threatened with his life if he tells. Can you imagine how the child feels and how his life has just flipped upside down? Where the hell was God, he would then ask as he grows up and egocentric thinking leaves his maturing mind. Have you ever thought of how an all seeing and knowing God would allow some things to happen and not stop them? I don't know about you, but I'm convinced some things will only be answered when we get to heaven.

I refused to be controlled by my past

I am a believer of the entire word of God to the point that it is not God's will for any of us to be controlled by our past. From what we've done or to what has been done to us, God's power can absolutely deliver. When you see people trapped in their past, it is usually because of one or two things. They haven't been exposed to deliverance, a deliverance ministry, or they have been in that sin or lifestyle so long that it is normal to them. Believe it or not, some Christians don't even really believe in deliverance despite how much the Bible talks about it. They believe the theory that "once in it always in it" and that is the biggest untruth this side of heaven. When people have never experienced deliverance and the power of Jesus Christ, they will always be stuck believing that they are destined to be gay, a player, a whorish woman, or a freak. What you believe is what you will be! You will have what you say.

> *"For as he thinketh in his heart, so is he."*
> *Proverbs 23:7 KJV,*

This is where many people will attack the pulpit and say, "Those preachers don't have power to deliver the people. Look at all these whoremongers, gays, and jacked up people in the church!" Have you ever considered some people enjoy the lifestyle they are living so they don't want to change? I preached a sermon that God gave me years ago in Louisville, Kentucky entitled "A slave that loves their chains will never be free." You have to hate a past lifestyle or it will remain your current lifestyle. No matter how many revivals, conventions or conferences you have, people will remain the bound that don't want to be free. It is like a person that is given a prescription from their doctor for a sickness that is curable. The person goes in the store, but never goes to the pharmacy to turn in the prescription and get their antidote. They go to the shoe section and the food section, but never to the pharmacy to get what they need. That is exactly how some people are when it comes to church. They want to be entertained and not changed. Don't let that be you.

The Greek word for healing is "soterio" which means salvation that is the avenue that leads to healing. It further means to restore to a state of wholeness after being broken and torn and to be completely delivered from the molestation of an enemy. Soterio also means to keep safe and sound from danger or destruction. When you put your life totally in Christ's hands, total deliverance will come. When you are in a ministry where you have a pastor who ministers to the total man, you are in a good place. It is sad to say that so many ministries only focus on having financial prosperity or a good relationship. You can be paid in full and still full of demons. You can be a Christian woman who is married to the best man yet you are the worst woman. Very few ministries will go deep enough into the real issues. I can't say it enough: deliverance is a major key for a fruitful life from a dreaded past.

Counseling with a professional and not just someone that has degrees from man's educational institutions, but also experienced in the spirit is very beneficial. Many broken pieces including emotional, physical, and even trust issues can be dealt with on a one on one basis. Now, don't get mad at this comment, but it's the truth. Some pastors or church leaders can only pray for you and not counsel with you because that is not their expertise. After putting oil on your head while you are at the altar and praying to God, that is as far as some can go and there is nothing wrong with that. Wrong counseling with the wrong counselor can actually trigger bad emotions and feelings that were meant to stay buried, so be sure to choose wisely. Wise counselors have the skill to take the individual back to the place mentally like the closet or basement to regather the broken pieces of their heart. For example, a certain individual who received good counseling went back to the basement of a family member's house where they were molested and was no longer haunted by the past! They began to speak to the broken them to come back and be whole. They told the hurt them to be healed. Finally, telling the weak them they are now strong! Now that is what I call total deliverance at its optimum!

The bounce-back factor

One of the greatest testimonies you can see and hear is, against all odds, someone going from the bottom to the top with the help of God. Surprisingly so many believe that those of sexual sins can never recover and be all God has called them to be. If that is the case, stop reading the Bible. From molestation, rape, and bad relationships, you have many survivors that have totally bounced back. You can't even tell they were once victims! When you hear their testimonies, you would almost think they are lying. To come out of the fire with no luggage or baggage is beautiful and it is an example of God's redemptive power.

This is one thing no one likes to hear, but everyday a marriage ends in divorce, everyday a person is molested or raped, and everyday a person's heart is broken by a so called Christian that used them like a dirty dish rag. At the same time, you might even be the person that I am talking about that has done these things. However, you yes even you can bounce back from having malicious behavior and become who God has always meant for you to be. The victim and the perpetrator can bounce back because God is just that bad. My soul is a witness!

I've learned on this page of my life and ministry to steer clear of people that have the propensity to make me miss out on my first class ticket to heaven while they sail to hell!

The following three points have put a smile on my face, hope in my heart and strength in my spirit:

1. Accept what has happened.

2. Let it go.

3. Believe the best is yet to come.

Destiny does not only work for the good things, but also for bad things. Some people were destined to go through things, while others were shielded because they couldn't handle it. One thing I will tell you as I close this book—strong people can handle anything. They are like eagles that can acclimate to their environment whether it is the heat from the jungle or the snow from winter. They rise! You have literally survived the worst season of your life and you are telling me that you don't think the best is yet to come? Walk tall, your chest out, your head high and shoulders squared because you've earned it. After going through what you have been through, regardless of what side of the fence you were on, can you imagined the look on the devil's face? He thought he had you, but you got away! You were not designed to simply endure pain and suffering but also joy and happiness. You, my friend, certainly qualify for years of smooth sailing on a boat named Peace. Sail on my friends and know that there is a victorious life after "Sex in the Pews".

ABOUT JONATHAN K. SANDERS

One of eight children born to Bishop Fred and Esther Sanders, Pastor Sanders realized there was a call on his life at a very early age. Even though the enemy planned to deter the young man from reaching his destiny, God's plan would ultimately prevail. After years of struggling with drugs, alcohol abuse and crime, the Lord would deliver him through a revival conducted by his father Apostle Fred Sanders, on September 28th, 1990 in Detroit, Michigan. "..For unto whomsoever much is given, of him shall be much required…" (Luke 12:48).

Pastor Sanders has been trusted to serve in many prestigious positions in ministry, and his most recent appointment is that of becoming the senior pastor of Victory Deliverance Church of Christ in Columbus, Ohio where his Father is the Presiding Prelate. Victory Deliverance Church, Inc. spans the United States, Caribbean Islands and Africa. In addition to serving as pastor of Victory Deliverance Church, he is also the founder and President of Victorious Living Ministries, a ministry that is designed to show the believer how to obtain victory in every area of their life.

Pastor Sanders received his bachelor's degree in Theology from Lighthouse Christian College, bachelor's degree in Psychology from the University of Phoenix and currently pursuing his Masters in Counseling. Pastor Sanders is a proud father of two sons who attend college in Florida. He stands on his favorite scripture is, "What shall we then say to these things? If God be for us, who can be against us? ~ Romans 8:31

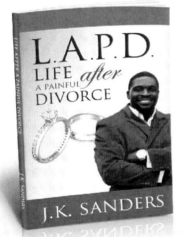